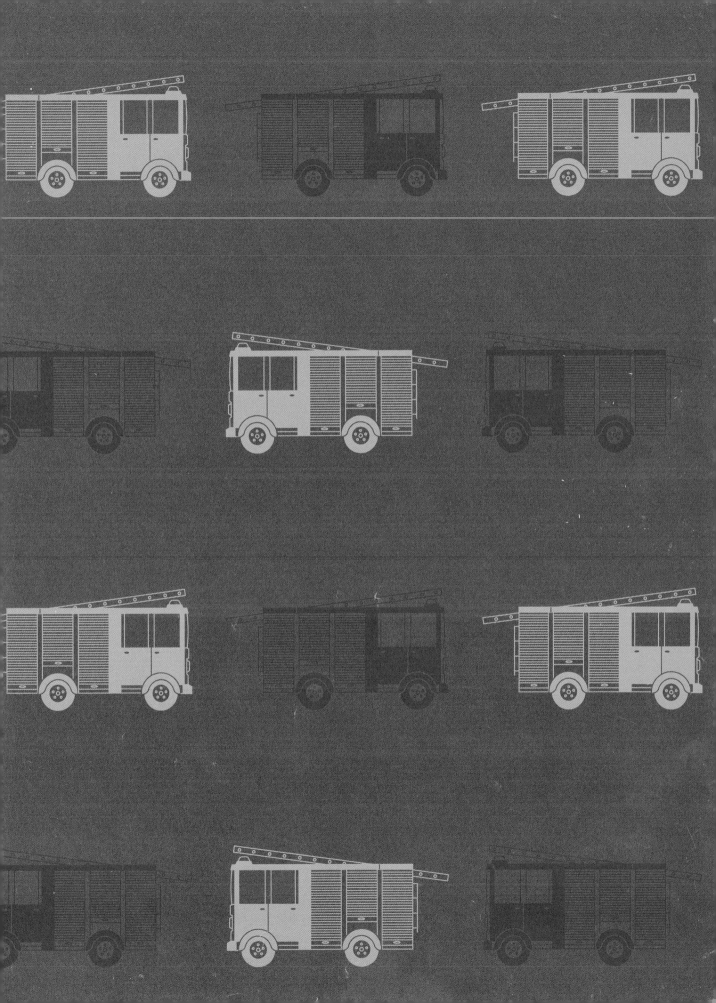

Fire Trucks

David and Penny Glover

Smart Apple Media

First published in 2004 by Franklin Watts
96 Leonard Street, London EC2A 4XD

Franklin Watts Australia
45-51 Huntley Street, Alexandria, NSW 2015

Series editor: Sarah Peutrill, Designer: Richard Langford, Art director: Jonathan Hair, Illustrator: Ian Thompson
Reading consultant: Margaret Perkins, Institute of Education, University of Reading

Picture credits: Dick Blume/Image Works/Topham: 15t. China Photo/Reuters/Corbis: 20b. Photo supplied by E-ONE (Ocala, Florida): 23b. Firepix/Topham: 6, 11b, 13b, 14t, 15b, 16. Hulton-Deutsch Collection/Corbis: 12. Photo courtesy of Mack Trucks Inc: 22c, 22b. Photo courtesy of Oshkosh Truck Corporation: 23t. PA/Topham: 21t. Mark Reinstein/Image Works/Topham: 7b. Reuters/Corbis: 21b. www.shoutpictures.com: front cover, 10, 11t, 18l, 18r. Watts Publishing: Chris Fairclough 4, 8t, 9b, 13t, 17t, 17b, 19t, 19b /Chris Honeywell 7t, 9t, 14b. Gloria Wright/Image Works/Topham: 8b.

Published in the United States by Smart Apple Media
2140 Howard Drive West, North Mankato, Minnesota 56003

Library of Congress Cataloging-in-Publication Data

Glover, David, 1953 Sept. 4-
Fire trucks / by David and Penny Glover.
p. cm. – (Big machines)
Includes index.
ISBN 1-58340-704-9
1. Fire engines–Juvenile literature. I. Glover, Penny. II. Title. III. Series.

TH9372.G657 2005
628.9'259–dc22   2004057863

Contents

To the rescue   6

Ready and waiting!   8

In the cab   10

Sirens and lights   12

Fire hoses   14

Ladders and booms   16

Rescue gear   18

Fire boats and planes   20

Giant fire trucks   22

Make it yourself   24

Trace your own fire truck   27

Fire truck words   28

Index   30

To the rescue

Fire trucks are big rescue machines. They carry firefighters to all kinds of emergencies.

A fire truck pumps water through its hoses to fight a fire. Its long ladder rescues people trapped in a burning building.

BIG FACT

A big fire truck is about 40 feet (12 m) long and 8 feet (2.5 m) wide.

At a car accident, firefighters cut people from crashed cars. The fire truck carries all the tools they need.

Fire trucks are painted bright colors. This is so they can be seen easily when they are racing to an emergency.

Ready and waiting!

The fire crew waits at the fire station for an emergency call.

The crew keeps the fire truck in perfect condition, ready to go at a moment's notice.

The fire truck is filled with diesel fuel. ▶

◀ The crew cleans the fire truck.

When an emergency call comes, the crew goes into action. Firefighters slide down a pole into the garage.

BIG FACT

There are more than one and a half million fires a year in the United States. That's one every 20 seconds.

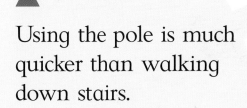

Using the pole is much quicker than walking down stairs.

The crew climbs aboard, the garage doors open, and the fire truck is on its way.

9

In the cab

The driver's cab has the same controls as other big road trucks.

Mobile telephone

Steering wheel

Control panel

Radio

Fax machine

The cab also has satellite navigation. This shows the fastest route to the emergency.

In most fire trucks, there are seats behind the driver. These are for the rest of the fire crew.

Some of the fire-fighters' equipment is kept next to their seats. ▲

At the emergency, it is important to keep in touch with the command center.

◄ A firefighter speaks to the command center using the cab's radio.

Sirens and lights

In the past, a fire truck had a bell to warn that it was coming. The firefighters held on to the sides as the truck raced along.

Bell

A bell is not loud enough for today's busy roads. A modern fire truck has a loud warning siren.

Siren

Light

The siren on this fire truck is between the warning lights.

A bright flashing light shows that the fire truck is near. People hear the siren, look for the light, and get out of the way.

At a fire, flashing lights warn people to keep away.

Fire hoses

At the fire, the firefighters reel out hoses to spray water onto the flames.

A hose is a hollow tube. A powerful pump pushes water out of the hose's nozzle.

Nozzle

Hose

The fire truck carries some water in a tank, but to fight a big blaze, it must pump water from a fire hydrant, a river, or a pond.

A firefighter unlocks a hydrant before attaching the hose.

Fire hydrant

A monitor is a powerful water cannon. It can be pointed by hand or operated by remote control.

A monitor ▶ pumps water from the top of a ladder onto a blazing house.

A monitor is operated by the crew on top of a fire truck. ▶

Ladders and booms

Ladders help firefighters fight fires in tall buildings.

The ladder operator uses the controls to raise the ladder and swing it into place.

The ladder on this fire truck is telescopic. Its sections slide over each other to make it longer.

This fire truck has a hydraulic boom. The boom unfolds to lift the platform high into the air.

Boom

Platform

Controls

A firefighter operates the boom from the bottom. ▶

A firefighter on the platform can make a rescue or spray water into a burning building.

Rescue gear

The fire truck's compartments are filled with all kinds of rescue gear. There is something for every kind of emergency.

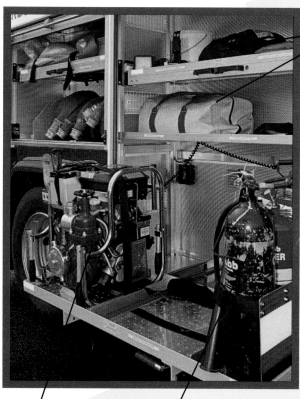

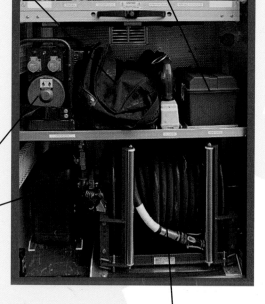

Chemical protection suits

Warning lights

Tool kits

Hydrant equipment

Spill bag
(to soak up chemicals)

Portable pump

Generator

Dry foam fire extinguishers

Blocks
(to put under cars to keep them from moving)

Hose

It is important to make sure all the equipment is in good working order.

A firefighter tests the breathing apparatus. ▶

◀ Two firefighters clean their chemical protection suits in a special shower.

Fire boats and planes

When a ship catches fire, a fire boat comes to the rescue. It pumps water from the sea to put out the flames.

Forest fires are the biggest fires of all. Planes and helicopters are needed to fight these huge blazes.

A fire helicopter flies over burning trees and drops a load of water from a bag onto the flames below.

A fire plane releases water from a tank. It can carry more than 1,320 gallons (5,000 l) at a time.

Giant fire trucks

The Super Pumper and Super Pumper Tender were the most powerful fire trucks ever built. They fought fires in New York City from 1965 to 1982.

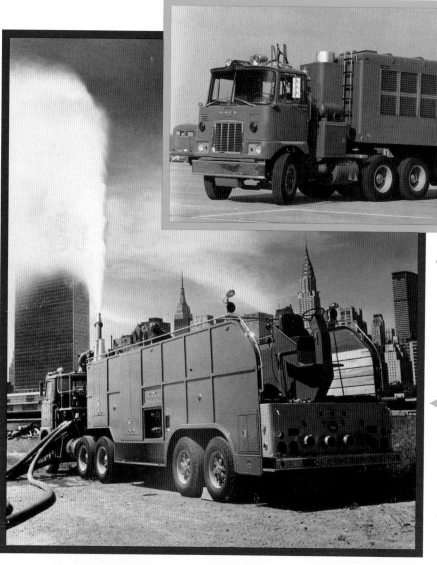

▲ The Super Pumper was used for very large fires.

◀ The water cannon on top of the Tender was very powerful. It could knock down thick walls.

The Striker 4500 is one of the most powerful fire trucks in the world today. It puts out fires at airports.

▲ Even though it weighs 55 tons (50 t), the Striker 4500 can speed across the runway at 70 miles (112 km) per hour on its eight wheels.

BIG FACT The boom on the Bronto F174 HDT can rise 174 feet (53 m) into the air.

Bronto boom

Make it yourself

Make a box model fire truck
with a telescopic ladder.

You will need:

An adult
to help

Paints

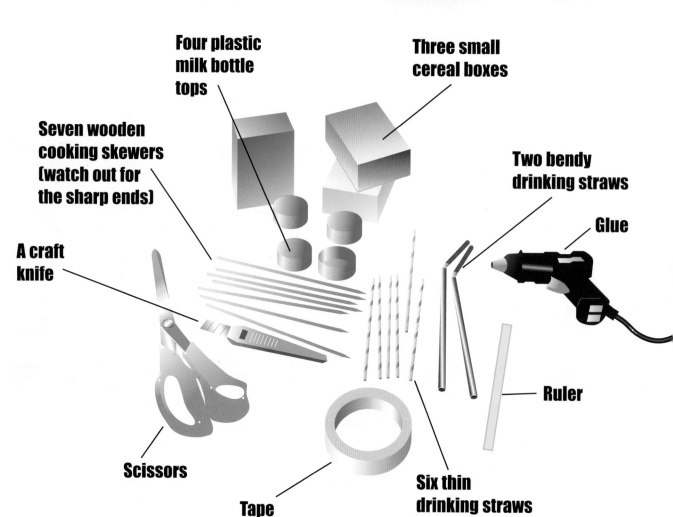

**Four plastic
milk bottle
tops**

**Three small
cereal boxes**

**Seven wooden
cooking skewers
(watch out for
the sharp ends)**

**Two bendy
drinking straws**

Glue

**A craft
knife**

Ruler

Scissors

**Six thin
drinking straws**

Tape

NOTE! Get an adult to help you with the cutting and glueing.

1. Cut 14 two-inch (5 cm) lengths of plastic straw and two four-inch (10 cm) lengths.

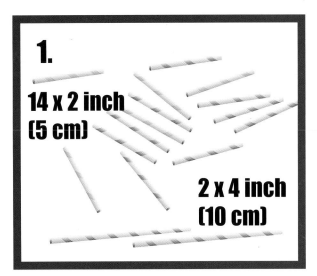

1.

14 x 2 inch (5 cm)

2 x 4 inch (10 cm)

2. Push a wooden skewer through one end of a short length of straw, as shown. The straw is a rung on the ladder.

2.

3.

3. Add six more rungs. Complete the ladder with a second skewer on the other side of the rungs.

Make a second ladder in the same way.

4. Bend down the ends of a four-inch (10 cm) length of straw to make it the same width as your ladder. Push the pointed ends of the skewers into the bends as shown. You can use the bent lengths of straw to join ladders together.

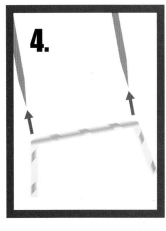

4.

5. Glue or tape the three boxes together to make the fire truck body.

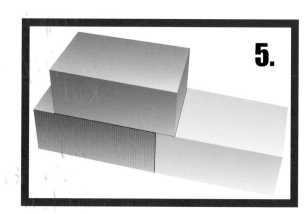

5.

6. Cut a slot at the back of the body for the ladder.

Push a skewer through the body and the straws at the bottom of one of the ladders. Make sure the hole is tight. Cut the skewer to length.

Use skewers and bottle tops to give your fire truck wheels as shown.

6.

8.

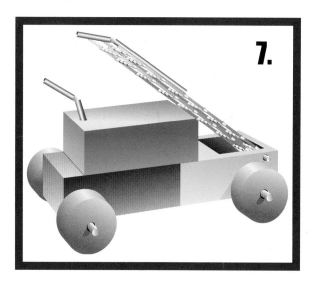

7.

7. Use bendy straws to add monitors (water cannons) to the top ladder section and the fire truck cab.

8. Raise the ladder on your fire truck!

Trace your own fire truck

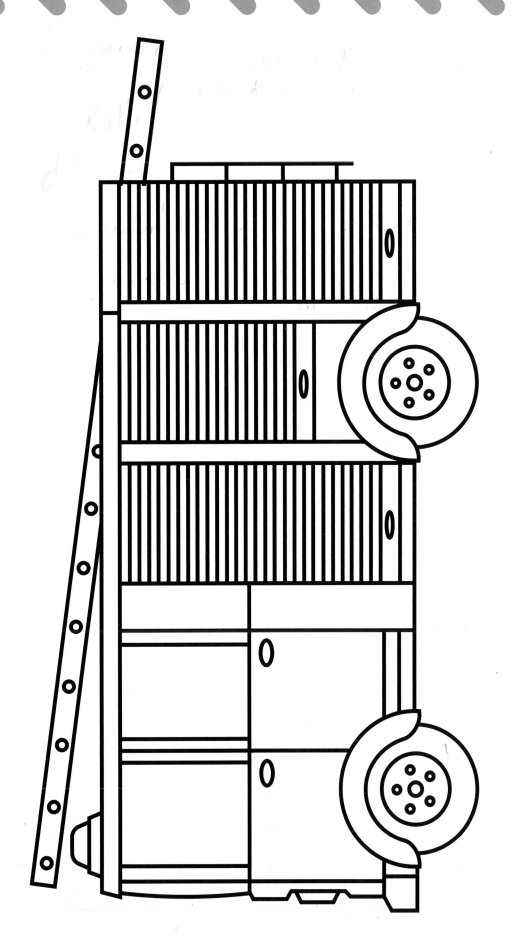

Fire truck words

cab
The part of the fire truck in which a driver sits.

chemical protection suit
A special full body suit worn by a firefighter to protect him or her from dangerous chemicals.

diesel
The fuel a fire truck uses to make it go.

firefighter
A member of a fire crew whose job is to fight fires.

fire hydrant
A pipe and nozzle joined to the water pipe under a road. A fire engine can get water from a hydrant to fight a fire.

hose

A flexible (bendy) tube for carrying water.

hydraulic boom

A mechanical arm that unfolds to reach high places. The force to raise the boom comes from hydraulic rams.

monitor

A powerful water cannon.

nozzle

The metal part on the end of a hose that is used to direct the water.

pump

A machine for making water or oil move through a pipe or hose.

satellite navigation

A computer map on a screen that shows where a fire engine is and the best route to an emergency.

siren

A machine that makes a very loud wailing sound.

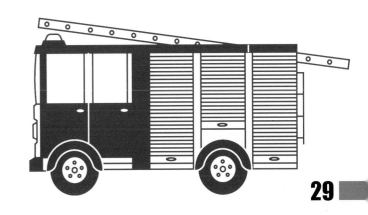

Index

bell 12, 13
boom, hydraulic 17, 29
breathing apparatus 19
Bronto F174 HDT 23

cab 10-11, 26, 28
car accident 7
chemical protection suit
        18, 19, 28
compartment 18

diesel 8, 28
driver 10

fire boat 20
fire helicopter 21
fire hydrant 14, 18, 28
fire plane 21
fire station 8
forest fire 21

hose 6, 14, 29

ladder 6, 15, 16, 24, 25, 26
light 13, 18

monitor 15, 26, 29

nozzle 14, 29

pole 9
pump 14, 18, 29

radio 10, 11

satellite navigation 29
siren 13, 29
steering wheel 10
Striker 4500 23
Super Pumper 22